NA'

NEW YORK
DIVORCE CASE

David I. Bliven

Speakeasy Publishing
73-03 Bell Blvd, #10
Oakland Gardens, NY 11364
www.speakeasypublishinginc.com

Ordering Information:

Quantity sales. Special discounts are available on quantity purchases by corporations, associations, and others. For details, contact the publisher at the address above.

Orders by U.S. trade bookstores and wholesalers. Please contact Speakeasy Publishing: Tel: (888) 991-2766 or visit www.speakeasypublishinginc.com.

Printed in the United States of America.

Published in 2018.

ISBN: 978-1-946481-23-8

FOREWORD

Statistically 50% of all marriages end in divorce[1]. And yet despite the often complex nature of divorce litigation, upwards of a majority of those who have divorce cases represent themselves[2].

This book is geared to both the pro se litigant (those who choose to represent themselves) as well as the person contemplating hiring an attorney. It's also useful for those you've already hired an attorney, and are looking for general knowledge as to "how my case is going to play out." Think of it this way – if you ask your attorney questions which this book provides answers to, s/he will charge you about $300-500 for this information. This book costs a fraction of that amount.

Because this book is geared to the litigants themselves, it will have a minimum of citations and footnotes. I want this book to come across as if you're sitting in my office and speaking to me. This book is more of a "how-to" guide and one which will arm you with knowledge – both to assist your own attorney as well as to assist yourself.

---

[1] http://www.apa.org/topics/divorce/
[2] http://iaals.du.edu/sites/default/files/documents/publications/cases_without_counsel_research_report.pdf.

While there are many resources out there containing articles to assist litigants[3], there are few known books which gather together much of the basic information one needs to know about the divorce process. As such, I sincerely want this book to help *you* – the divorcing person – make sense of the divorce process during one of the most stressful times of your life.

I must add that my experience over the past 20 years is mostly within courts in the greater New York City area (including Westchester and Long Island). While many of the ideas and procedures I relate in this book are transferable across the many jurisdictions of New York, one should note that practice does vary amongst counties – and even between judges in a particular courthouse. As such, nothing beats the advice of a well-experienced matrimonial who has practiced for many years in the county where your case is in.

---

[3]http://family.findlaw.com/divorce.html,
http://family-law.lawyers.com/divorce/,
http://www.nycourts.gov/divorce/index.shtml

DISCLAIMER

This publication is intended to be used for educational purposes only. No legal advice is being given, and no attorney-client relationship is intended to be created by reading this material. The author assumes no liability for any errors or omissions or for how this book or its contents are used or interpreted or for any consequences resulting directly or indirectly from the use of this book. For legal or any other advice, please consult an experienced attorney or the appropriate expert.

The Law Offices of David Bliven
www.blivenlaw.net

White Plains Office

445 Hamilton Avenue

Suite 607

White Plains, NY 10601

(914) 468-0968

Bronx Office

3174 Riverdale Avenue

Suite 1

Bronx, NY 10463

(718) 725-9600

TABLE OF CONTENTS

INTRODUCTION:
CONTEMPLATING A DIVORCE?

When contemplating a divorce, people often have problems facing the prospect of paying alimony and maintenance, or they're looking to get alimony and maintenance. So, there's really a worry of how much they are going to get, and how soon they are going to get it.

If one is the prospective payer, one worries about how much of a bite it's going to take out of their wallet. For example, in New York there are "maintenance guidelines," which result in the "general rule" of an alimony award. Unfortunately, in some cases these guidelines are unfair. For example, in order to determine the amount that a payor will have to pay, the Judge will often look at presumptive guidelines based on the sheer calculation of their income irrespective of what expenses they have. Expenses largely do not come into the mix in calculating the presumptive maintenance that they will have to pay (see more on this in Chapter 9).

To clarify, in New York "maintenance" is another word for "alimony." So, in some cases - especially once combined with a child support award - this can result in maintenance being approximately 50% to 60% of someone's take-home pay. I often face cases where the person (and it's usually the husband, though certainly not always) is either looking to move out, or has already established residence elsewhere. They are looking at the expenses they have to commit to - such as rent, food, utilities and things of that nature. Many people are spending an inordinate percentage of their income on housing, especially in the greater New York City area, which includes Westchester.

Oftentimes, housing comprises 30% to 40% of someone's take-home pay in this area, and the problem is that a lot of people commit this percentage of income to a housing expense when they are living together as an intact family unit. When they get divorced and split up that family unit, each spouse is committing to a separate housing expense which separately comprises 30% to 40% of their take-home pay. Oftentimes, the numbers just don't add up – resulting in both parties to a divorce feeling squeezed.

I review "monthly budgets" with clients in which they have committed to a mortgage on a marital residence - and they have to keep paying at least a percentage of that mortgage *even when they move out*. On top of that, they have to commit to paying rent or a mortgage someplace else. As such, many times when people do their budget *as an intact family* (i.e., before they split up consequent to the divorce) they have (maybe) about $1,000 to $3,000 left-over at the end of each month - just as spending money or petty cash.

That's precisely where the problem comes in. Once they split up the family and they are no longer an intact unit, if the husband (and I use the husband which, again, is not always the case) begin living on his own by establishing residence elsewhere, he's going to spend somewhere in the neighborhood of $1,500 to $2,000 a month on rent alone. If he only had $3,000 left over at the end of each month after paying the expenses when they were an intact family unit, one can see half of that money (or more) is now gone just in rent. So now, instead of paying 30% to 40% of his take-home pay for housing, he is paying more in the neighborhood of 50% to 60% of his take-home pay on housing for himself.

Once you add in a separate food bill, separate utilities, transportation, and (in some cases) credit card debt, they easily have to spend about $4,000 to $5,000 a month. Then, the problem becomes being able to afford the maintenance and child support payments.

Likewise, the person who stays in the home may very well have legitimate concerns about the spouse who has just moved out of the house, leaving them with expenses of $2,000-$3,000 a month for mortgage, food, utilities, and other basics for themselves and usually one or two kids. How will that spouse make ends meet if they are no longer receiving money from the spouse who moved out?

As a result, oftentimes there is extreme pressure on behalf of *both* the prospective recipient of maintenance *and* the payor to make ends meet on a basic level. On top of that, you have to figure out the appropriate amount of maintenance and child support.

A lot of times, I suggest right at the outset of a case that my client draft a monthly budget, looking at what their net income is - and figure out from there what they can afford (if need be). On the recipient's end, they need to determine what they need in order to make ends meet. Doing a monthly budget - which I often assist with - looks so much better to the matrimonial judge if a motion has to be filed on the issue. This is because you can literally put that on a spreadsheet right into your motion, and make it very visual for the judge. The judge will see that we aren't asking for "pie in the sky" numbers; we're actually asking for exactly what is needed for the recipient. In dealing with a payer's budget, we are demonstrating exactly what they can afford to pay while still meeting basic minimum expenses on their end.

It's rare that a judge will look someone in the face and say, "Look, you have these basic expenses, you can't really cut them at all, but we are still going to make you pay a combination of maintenance and child support that is going to exceed what you need in order to pay rent and to eat." So, a lot of times this is the tension, at least in regards to alimony on the divorce end. Certainly there are also property and asset issues, but oftentimes it's not as urgent of an issue at the outset of the case.

However, you do have issues where one spouse is in the process of selling property that is only in their name, and the other spouse wants to stop that process or at least have the sales proceeds put in escrow pending completion of the divorce process. Luckily, in New York, we have automatic orders[4] that go into place when a divorce case is filed, stating that presumptively marital property will not be sold or transferred during the process of the divorce case.

The tension then becomes defining the marital and separate property. Can someone sell premarital property or property that is clearly only in their name? If they purport to sell that property, it's an arguable violation of the automatic orders which would then require litigation before a judge to decide the issue.

I've certainly had clients come to me where the parties have attempted to do things on their own. Let's say

---

[4]http://www.nycourts.gov/divorce/forms_instructions/Notice.pdf.

they sold property and the sales proceeds get deposited into a joint account. Then, when one spouse or the other sees the divorce coming, they'll go into that divorce account and take either their share of the amount, or the entire amount.

The problem - which is something I've faced - is that some judges will say that it is a trial issue. In other words, the one spouse who is now deprived of that money going into the divorce case, has to file an interim motion asking that the divorce judge divide that amount in half, giving each spouse one half. It's completely discretionary on the part of the divorce judge to do that before a trial is held.

I had one case where the parties sold a condo in Manhattan and received approximately $200,000 to $250,000 in sales proceeds. They deposited that money into a joint account, and the wife took every penny out of that account and put it in her own account.

When the husband in that case hired me, we went in with guns blazing before the divorce judge and said we want half of that money. That's only fair. Unfortunately, the divorce judge in that case said, "I'm not going to do anything about it before trial, that's a trial issue." The problem was further complicated because the wife had to pay $200,000 or more to her attorney, and my client had no money at all to pay me.

To make a long story short, he ended up having to settle for a less than ideal settlement because he ran out of money to finish the litigation. She continued to have plenty of money to fund the litigation.

So, if there is a joint account involved, I often advise my potential clients to withdraw their share as soon as possible, because you do not want to rely on the other spouse's good faith. You don't want to *hope* s/he will only take their fair share of the joint account. Sometimes it works like that and sometimes it doesn't. It's a huge gamble if it doesn't work out that way.

All that said, one can see there are many thickets divorce litigation can get into. This book is intended to be an introductory guide to act as a "roadmap" through your case. It is not intended to take the place of having competent legal counsel at your side at every step of the way!

****

Chapter 1 (What are the options?) will provide an overview of the different filing options and ways to proceed. Chapter 2 will walk you through the divorce process – and give you a picture of how your case may proceed. Chapter 3 will address common misunderstandings as to "how divorces go."

Chapter 4 will review how assets are generally divided in a divorce case – as well as ways to protect one's assets. Chapter 5 will discuss how spousal maintenance (a/k/a alimony) is handled in New York.

Chapters 7 and 8 discuss the issues of child support, custody & visitation and family offense (orders of protection). These chapters will be relatively brief as they will be expanded upon in a forthcoming book on the Family Court process – the issues are virtually the same whether they are addressed in Family Court or within the context of a divorce proceeding.

Finally, Chapter 9 will provide guidance in how to go about selecting a divorce attorney. Suffice it to say, lawyers are not like doctors – they vary widely in their expertise and ability to handle complex matters. Using this book will hopefully make you a savvy shopper.

I wish to add one final proviso - if you dare you represent yourself, do not make this book your last stop. Take a trip over to the Supreme Court library in your county and begin educating yourself. I recommend reading a treatise on divorce law such as NEW YORK LAW OF DOMESTIC RELATIONS by Alan D. Scheinkman[5]. Moreover, if your case involves Domestic Violence issues, you'd do well to review NEW YORK LAW OF DOMESTIC VIOLENCE by Melissa L. Breger, Hon. Lee H. Elkins and Jane Fosbinder[6]. Finally, if your case is heading to trial, familiarize yourself with EVIDENCE IN NEW YORK STATE AND FEDERAL COURTS by Robert A. Barker and Vincent C. Alexander[7].

While this may be a daunting task, books like these serve as a starting point (beyond law school & years of experience) which good divorce attorneys use to "get up to speed" on divorce law basics (not to mention countless hours of lectures at continuing legal education seminars). *Especially* if you elect to represent yourself and the other side is represented, reviewing treatises like these are

---

[5] West Publishing (2012).
[6] West Publishing (2016).
[7] West Publishing (2012).

probably the least you could do to not risk substantial damage on your case.

But word to the wise – "one who represents oneself has a fool for a client." At the least, you should schedule a consultation appointment with a capable attorney in your area – educate yourself, then decide for yourself who is best to proceed.

CHAPTER 1
WHAT ARE THE OPTIONS?

Is it better to merely get a legal separation, or proceed with filing a divorce case?

Prior to October, 2010, one generally needed to make an allegation of fault against his/her spouse in order to get divorced. One common way around that was to do a separation agreement. The law provided that if the parties remained separated pursuant to a Separation Agreement for more than 1 year, then either could thereafter file for an uncontested divorce based on the agreement. This indeed was one of the leading reasons why people prior to the law's amendment filed for separation as opposed to divorce.

Now that New York has passed "No-Fault" Divorce, however, there is no longer any reason to allege fault in order to get divorced - one only needs to state that the marriage has broken down "irretrievably" for more than 6 months. This is roughly the equivalent of what many other states call "irreconcilable differences."

Once the parties are divorced, then generally if one is covered by his/her spouse's medical insurance, their insurance will terminate. This is because very few plans cover "ex-spouses." As such, a leading reason why some people still choose to get a legal separation first is to preserve continuity of insurance coverage for at least another year.

With the Separation Agreement, the parties can resolve every other issue which would otherwise be brought up in the divorce. The agreement would cut-off accrual of marital assets & debts, and can equitably divide them. The agreement can also provide for custody, visitation, maintenance (i.e., alimony) & child support. The only thing the agreement cannot do is actually terminate the marriage. That takes a divorce proceeding - which either party can file for upon the expiration of 1 year (or later) from the date the agreement is signed.

****

Another option that people have right at the outset of a divorce process is choosing mediation - versus hiring their own attorneys to try to negotiate a settlement. Mediation does work in some cases - statistically, it results in a full resolution of the case about 50% of the time[8], and it can save people money and stress. If you only retain 1 attorney for both people, you'll pay approximately half as much as each of you would pay for having your own separate attorney.

Even in cases where people do mediation, it's still recommended they have their own attorney "waiting in the wings." You'll still go through the mediation process - meaning you will sit down with the mediator for about two or three sessions and attempt to come up with the basic terms of the settlement. However, you want your own attorney waiting in the wings so you can go back to that attorney and ask them questions about what the mediator

---

[8] http://www.nycourts.gov/ip/adr/CaseOutcomes.shtml.

has said during the process, and whether or not it is a fair settlement. Those are questions the mediator cannot answer for any particular party. They are not there to give legal advice, nor are they there to say whether or not a settlement is fair to a particular party. So, a lot of times I have parties that go through mediation and hire me simultaneously, so they have their own attorney that they can come back to.

Now, with respect to mediation, the unfortunate thing is when it doesn't work, the parties actually end up spending *more money* than if they had just gone with their own attorneys to negotiate a settlement from the beginning. The reason is because if you paid $5,000 for a mediator, and mediation doesn't work, then that money is gone. On top of that cost, each party must hire their own attorney and spend an additional $5,000-$10,000+. A failed mediation can also result in the parties spending a lot more time on the whole process, because many attorneys will start from scratch.

So, the other obvious option that people have is to simply hire their own attorneys. A lot of times the process of settlement negotiation will involve the parties exchanging net worth statements[9] at the outset, which are simply sworn statements that set forth income, expenses, assets and liabilities.

The net worth statement then serves as a starting point to negotiate a fair settlement on both ends. A lot of times after the net worth statements are changed, the attorneys will then get together either via email or via phone and discuss what each respective party is seeking in terms of settlement. Then, they'll see how far apart they are on settlement. Sometimes they are not far apart at all. Sometimes the attorneys will agree on pretty much everything because the parties have pretty much agreed on everything. If so, then one attorney or the other will draft a settlement agreement (which is usually a 20-30+ page document). The parties will sign it and they will essentially be done.

If the parties are very far apart on some issues, then the attorneys will negotiate with each other and go back to their respective parties. They will tell them where they are

---

[9] See this link for the official form:
http://www.nycourts.gov/FORMS/matrimonial/Net%20Worth%20 Statement%20Form%20(Gender%20Neutral)%20rev.%20June%202016 %20Eff.%208.1.16.pdf.

at in the negotiation process, and ask them whether or not they are willing to give in a little on a particular issue.

Oftentimes, I will tell clients there is the law - and there is also just plain cost-benefit analysis. For example, a lot of times a spouse - especially if it's the less-monied spouse - will make a claim to an asset that they are clearly not entitled to. Let's say it's a clearly premarital property, the non-titled spouse didn't make any investments in the property during the marriage, and maybe it's even a short-term marriage. They have no kids together, but the spouse still says they want a piece of that property, and that they don't care what the law says.

My client will go to me and say, "Well Dave, what do you think about that?" I'll tell them that the law completely supports them. If it's premarital property, her name isn't on the title, she didn't invest in it, you have no kids, and there are no other factors that justify her getting a share of that property, then the law will generally support you.

However, the problem is often that the opposing party is not obligated to settle. There is no way an attorney can force a settlement on the other side, no matter how well justified the legal argument. If she wants to contest the case, you are looking at paying $10,000+ to go in front of a Judge on a contested case. Then, from a pure cost-benefit analysis, is it actually worth it to you to offer $5,000 or some other amount, just to make the issue go away? Even if it's not right in the law, it may actually end up saving them money, which is kind of the point of the issue.

If I can save money for a client, I'll advise them to put their feelings and their sense of justice aside. I'll advise them to save that money for another day, or give that money to your ex-spouse and the mother of your children in order to make the issue go away and wrap things up.

****

There are instances in which one spouse is the "breadwinner" of the family - and then abruptly leaves the marital residence and refuses to support the family. The remaining spouse should have a game-plan on what options to choose from.

While often times if people are getting a divorce anyway, the knee-jerk reaction is to file for divorce. If there are emergency issues, however - such as how the rent/mortgage going is to be paid this month - then filing a motion in Supreme Court may not be the way to go. This is because Supreme Court is often slow in deciding such issues. Even on an emergency motion the court gets up to 60 days to decide the motion - and that's from when all papers have been submitted by both sides (which especially in NYC & surrounding counties can take 1-2+ months in itself). In other words, if you need a quick order, filing a motion in Supreme Court may cost you 4-5+ months just to get a decision - and even that's on an emergency motion.

Generally, the courts do not want the same issue pending in two courts at the same time. In other words, Judges would otherwise frown on the same party filing for divorce in Supreme Court & including a maintenance (i.e. alimony) claim while simultaneously filing a spousal support case in Family Court. However, one major exception is where the party requesting support is "in danger of becoming a public charge" - in other words, without the Court ordering the other side to pay support, the "needy" spouse would otherwise need to apply for some form of public assistance (food stamps, rent assistance, etc.) in order to pay their basic bills.

In Family Court, one can get an initial court date within 4-6 weeks of filing one's support petition - and therefore usually get some form of support order entered in far less time than it would generally take for Supreme Court to decide the support issue. As such, if emergency support is needed, the requesting party should strongly consider proceeding in Family Court first (of course after consultation with an experienced Family Law attorney)!

****

Filing First For Divorce

A final "option" is really a non-option – which party should file first. There aren't any direct advantages or disadvantages to filing first for divorce. The filer pays the court fees, and strategically speaking, I sometimes find that it's better to be the defendant. I often analogize it to Muhammad Ali's rope-a-dope fight, where he kind of leaned against the ropes and let the other person attack him. He found that it was actually strategic to ward off the attack while taking jabs & leaning against the ropes. He actually won that fight because he allowed the attack to exhaust itself. In the divorce context, I sometimes don't mind if the other side has to put on their entire case first, because then I get to see exactly what they are coming at and the full range of their attack. By having this knowledge, I am better able to plan my defense on every single issue before going on the attack myself.

The other side won't have the opportunity to plan their defense as effectively as I was able to. Sometimes I like that, but there are also cases where people will come to me, especially if they are the more moneyed spouse. I have to advise them that any delay in filing just pushes back the cutoff date of the accrual of marital assets. So, if they are the more moneyed spouse and they are continuing to invest money into investment accounts or retirement accounts, delaying the filing by several months just means several more months of accrual of marital assets that they will end up having to share. So it's kind of a Catch-22. Other than that, there is really no advantage or disadvantage to filing first.

CHAPTER 2
DIVORCE PROCESS – A BRIEF TIMELINE

A typical flow of the uncontested case will start with the filing of the case. You can either file with a summons with notice or a summons & complaint. I have always filed my divorce cases as summons & complaint, simply because the complaint is the actual "pleading" that you'll need to get divorced. The summons with notice is similar to putting someone on notice that you are filing for divorce. It's filed with the county clerk's office in any given supreme court where the party resides.

The current filing fee as of 2017 is $210. Then, the filer has up to 120 days presumptively to serve the other side with the summons in complaint. You can do via either formal service or informal service. Formal service means you have a licensed process server attempt to serve them. Informal service means that either my client gives the other person the papers, or I email or mail it to them. Informal service requires his/her signature or an acknowledgement that they've actually received the summons, while formal service does not. So, if they are formally served by a licensed process server, you no longer need his/her signature or consent. If your spouse formally answers the summons, then a lot of times it means they've hired an attorney, though not always.

Once they answer the summons on an uncontested, the attorneys commence settlement negotiation and hope to resolve the case. From the point that the defendant files his/her answer to the complaint, the law gives another 120 days to presumptively negotiate a settlement. After the 120 days have passed, the law essentially encourages the filing of a contested case. At any point, however, either party can trigger a contested case. As such, if either party thinks the settlement negotiation isn't going to result in a successful settlement, s/he can trigger a contested case any time before the 120-days lapses. If you exceed the 120-days because you were actively negotiating a settlement (which ended up being successful), in my experience no court is going to reject the divorce just because you exceeded the 120 days.

There are certainly cases where you attempt to serve the other side within that 120-day window, but you are not successful in doing so. Then the issue becomes, is the person found and you are not able to effectuate service? Or, is the other side's whereabouts unknown? If a server attempts service a number of times and is able to verify they have the correct location, then you can apply to the court for a "substituted service." This usually means a server will be authorized by the judge to leave a copy of the summons at the door, and then mail it to them - that's still considered "good service."

If the server is *not* successful in verifying your spouse is actually at the address you thought they were, then there's a need to hire a private investigator to look for the person and attempt to get a good address for the person. The private investigator will either be successful or not. If they are not successful in that process, then they will produce a diligent search report. This report will then be submitted to the judge with the request that the judge approve publication notice. Before one goes the route of a publication notice, one is highly encouraged to exhaust every single avenue one can possibly think of to locate a good address (even if it's an email address or a Facebook address). If one can locate something, one may able to get cooperation in effectuating service.

If one can't find the spouse anywhere, then the only other thing a court can do is to authorize publication notice. Unfortunately, here in New York, publication notice means running a copy of the summons in the legal notices section of the newspaper. Oftentimes (especially in the greater NYC-area) Judges approve either the Daily News or New York Times - which will run a party somewhere in the neighborhood of $6,000 to $8,000. So, it's an extremely expensive procedure - and that is why I highly encourage all of my clients to exhaust every single avenue before they have to go down that road.

****

31

If you need money to pay for your attorney, pay large bills, etc., you're best advised to secure those funds before the divorce is even filed. Once the case is filed, as stated, you may be restrained from accessing certain funds without consent of your spouse. As such, if there's a house which needs to be sold, go ahead & sell it (with, of course, the consent of your spouse) before the case is even filed. If there is a dispute as to credits owed to 1 party, or debts which need to be paid, then evenly split the undisputed funds & place the remainder in the escrow account of 1 of the attorneys.

If you have a large amount of money in a bank account, or investment account, you can handle it the same way. Split the undisputed money evenly, and any remaining funds you can either leave it in the joint account, or deposit it in 1 of the attorneys' escrow accounts. I have handled far too many cases in which the parties do not do this, then file their divorce case - only to discover they cannot then access the joint funds to pay for their attorney or pay large bills. Better to act now than pay your attorneys to fight it out!

****

After service of the initial paperwork is complete, the "defendant" usually serves either an Answer and/or a "Notice of Appearance." Bear in mind the "requested relief" (claims specified in the complaint) are usually just "boilerplate," umbrella terms, and are mere reservation of the filer's rights to pursue such claims. This "ancillary relief" section in the complaint does not constitute the filer's settlement offer.

In any event, after the "pleadings" are served (pleadings are the complaint & the Answer), then the attorneys (on behalf of their respective clients) attempt to negotiate a settlement of the case. As described briefly in Chapter 1, the attorneys will go back-and-forth between themselves and their clients to see if a middle ground can be reached on all possible claims. If it can, then it results in a settlement agreement, which is usually a 20-50+ page document resolving all possible issues between the parties. One attorney or the other then completes the "judgment package"[10] and then submits the package to the Court for the Judge's signature.

If the attorneys are unsuccessful in negotiating a settlement – meaning there's a disagreement on 1 or more issues – then either party may "contest" the case (as described below).

****

Contested Case

I will also very briefly go through the process of a contested case.

A contested case is where - at some point in the negotiation process - one party or the other does not think the negotiations will end in a settlement. They file what's called a "request for judicial intervention," which is just a long way of requesting that a judge be assigned to the case. With this filing, a court will schedule the initial court date called the "preliminary conference."

---

[10]
http://www.nycourts.gov/divorce/divorce_withchildrenunder21.shtml#ucdforms.

At the preliminary conference, especially in New York City and the greater NYC area, generally the attorneys will meet first with the Judge's Court Attorney (or Referee), which is similar to the Judge's "right-hand man/woman." This initial meeting is usually just with the attorneys present - though in some counties (e.g., Westchester) the parties may be involved at even this initial meeting. The Court Attorney/Referee will discuss settlement issues and make settlement suggestions.

The Court Attorney/Referee will also set up a discovery schedule, which is a formal exchange of financial documents and information. The court will also determine whether or not various forensic experts will be needed. If custody or visitation is an issue, they will decide whether or not to appoint an attorney for the child or children. They'll also certainly discuss what issues are being contested, and how far apart the parties are on settlement negotiations. Oftentimes, the judge or the referee will make settlement suggestions to the parties to try and bridge the gap. If a settlement is not in the cards at a preliminary conference, then the court will set up what is commonly called a compliance conference, which is just a date to come back to make sure that all the discovery has been exchanged, and that all the forensic reports are in. [11]

Additionally, if one party or the other is seeking interim relief – either an interim order of spousal maintenance or child support, an interim order than the other side pat for his/her attorney's fees, or an order of protection - the requesting party must generally file this motion for it to be hear at the preliminary conference. While at times a Judge may overlook this rule, one should not count on it happening in your case.

In contested cases, people often do depositions of both parties, and sometimes third parties. Depositions are where the parties are grilled under oath in the opposing attorney's conference room (with a reporter present). Some of the advantages in doing them are that they serve to lock in a party's testimony (so the attorney isn't questioning a witness for the first time at trial), and to learn information one cannot glean from financial documents themselves.

---

[11] See an expanded version of what goes on at a preliminary conference by referring to the court's rule - 22 NYCRR §202.16(f) - http://www.nycourts.gov/rules/trialcourts/202.shtml#16.

Oftentimes depositions are held off on until the very end of the case, simply because they are extremely expensive to do. I usually tell my clients that in order to do a deposition, they are looking at a $5,000 cost. I don't want to incur this cost for them unless it seems like we've exhausted every other avenue and we just can't settle the case. If the case still can't settle, they'll usually set up deposition dates at the compliance conference. If we still can't settle at the final court date (called a "pre-trial conference"), all the discovery has been exchanged and all the forensic reports are in, then the Judge will schedule a trial.

Short of depositions, many times parties do "demands for discovery & inspection," which is simply a demand to produce financial documents. As the law provides for a "extensive exchange of financial information," one can expect to exchange several years' worth of records, such as tax returns, bank account statements and credit card statements.

Additionally, parties to a contested case often do "interrogatories," which is just a list of questions the party must answer "under oath." Collectively these tools are called "disclosure."

If either party fails to provide the disclosure to the other side, or the production is inadequate, the requesting party may file a "motion to compel disclosure," which is a request that the Judge review their request and order (under threat of sanction) that the other side produce the missing disclosure by a certain deadline. Most of the time, however, the Court will want the movant to document his/her attempts to resolve the issues without the necessity of filing the motion[12].

Notably, these attorney's tools are rather limited in discovering hidden income or assets. Ultimately, a party alleging hidden income or assets may need to hire a private investigator or – depending on the nature of the income/assets – a forensic accountant.

As mentioned, beyond the "preliminary conference," the court usually conducts 2 other conferences – the compliance conference and the pre-trial conference (though any of these conferences may be adjourned more than once).

---

[12] Indeed, some courts such as Westchester require the attorney to first have a conference with the Referee prior to filing the motion.

In brief, the "compliance conference" is merely the "middle-of-the-road" conference to check on the status of exchange of disclosure, and to set further deadline dates for disclosure and/or dates of depositions.

At a "pretrial conference" date, the parties will have to submit - among other things - a proposed statement of disposition, updated net worth statements, and in a growing number of courts (including Westchester), they have to submit what is called a "trial notebook." A trial notebook essentially consists of pre-tabbed exhibits that each party intends to put into evidence - along with witness lists. It is very costly to put together a trial notebook, and oftentimes people are at the end of litigation at that point. Those fees mount really fast when parties are looking at doing a trial, and this is problematic if the parties are in need of money and do not have incomes that are well into the six-figures.

In that case, I usually have a discussion with clients - bringing them back to the cold hard cost-benefit analysis. If we are off in the negotiations by $10,000, $20,000 or even $30,000 (i.e., the difference between 1 party's settlement offer & the other's), then between paying my fees to do a trial as well as the other costs associated with it, some people may actually be better to offer his/her spouse the money than to give it to the attorney. Although the attorney's wallet is always open to accept donations, oftentimes it's better to offer the other side that money and make the issue go away. This is because you are going to have to spend the money anyway, and you'll either win on the issue or you'll lose. Either way, you will have still have spent $10,000, $20,000 or $30,000 (or more) paying the attorney. On top of that, you will still face the prospect of spending the same amount of money if you lose on the issue, whether it involves asset division or a maintenance issue.

That's pretty much the flow of a contested case. You are looking at approximately three to five pretrial court dates, and typical trials are usually conducted between approximately two and five trial dates.

Preliminary Conference

Compliance Conference

Pre-Trial Conference

Chapter 3
MISCONCEPTIONS ABOUT THE DIVORCE PROCESS

One of the most common misunderstandings about the divorce process is the issue of title.

Oftentimes people have retirement assets, bank accounts or even property that's in their sole name. Because of that, they think the asset is theirs. The problem is that the divorce laws in New York actually say the opposite - title is not generally what the court looks at in dividing property. The overriding issue is whether or not the property was acquired during the marriage. Thus, if the property or asset was acquired during a marriage, then it is presumptively marital property irrespective of whose name is on the account or deed. In addition, if an asset actively accrues value during the marriage, that value - or what the law calls appreciation in the value of that account - is also generally marital property.

****

Some parties have money in bank accounts or assets in a portfolio and are now contemplating a divorce. How should they proceed?

First, New York has Automatic Orders which go into place upon the filing of a divorce. Thus, you cannot generally transfer or extinguish funds in a joint account after the filing unless your spouse consents. Money in the bank may be accessed for "usual & customary expenses," which generally entails household bills. If you're contemplating a divorce, it may behoove you to consult a Divorce Attorney now regarding what funds you can & cannot transfer.

Generally, assets one accrues prior to the marriage are one's "separate property." This means your spouse cannot ordinarily claim a right to such funds. However, the initial burden to prove a given asset is "separate" is on the holder of those assets. As such, you're best advised to start gathering the financial institution's statements which prove what funds or assets you held on the date of your marriage.

****

People may not realize their financial accounts are being "actively appreciated" during a marriage.

The common example is with either a pension or a 401(k) account. Thus, people often think that since it is *their account* with *their employer*, then their spouse doesn't get to share in the asset. Unfortunately, they're wrong. The problem is even if they had the pension or 401(k) account going into the marriage, any investment either by them or their employer into their account during the marriage is considered marital, such that the other spouse can claim a share of the account. Oftentimes it's 50% of the marital portion of that account.

Many times, this not only raises eyebrows, but causes great stress on behalf of the moneyed spouse who has investment accounts. They feel it's unfair! They feel like: "I had the foresight to invest money into my retirement, she didn't save a penny, and now you're telling me she gets half?!?"

It may be true his/her spouse didn't do anything at all in regards to retirement, and didn't even set up an IRA or 401(k). Maybe the other spouse haphazardly spent money on frivolous things during marriage, and as a result s/he has no assets at all when the divorce is filed. The other spouse was wise, used foresight and invested tens of thousands or hundreds of thousands of dollars into retirement accounts, only to learn that in a divorce case, half of that money simply belongs to the spouse who didn't bother to put any money aside.

Then I have to explain to them the concept of "marital money." Marital money is essentially any money which either one of them earns *from any source* during their marriage. Oftentimes people think "while I'm earning money from my job, that money is mine. After all, I earned it - my name is on the paycheck!"

I have to dispel this misconception. Once you say "I Do," you have formed an economic partnership. And once you form an economic partnership, one partner to the partnership could be extremely enterprising and earn a lot of money, but basic partnership law says when you dissolve a partnership, everything is generally divisible 50/50.

Once things are divisible 50/50, the spouse that didn't contribute anything to the partnership is still presumptively entitled to 50% of that which was accrued during the marriage. That will include situations in which one spouse has marital money from a job, rental income, or investment income. Once they take that money and invest it into financial accounts - whether those are retirement accounts, bank accounts, stocks, bonds, mutual funds, etc. - it is converted to assets. And it's the *assets* that the court actually looks to in deciding what to divide between the spouses. So, it's usually the assets that are most contested (other than custody issues) in a divorce case because of that raw feeling of unfairness.

****

Often a share of significant assets can turn on the precise definition of what constitutes "marital property" versus "separate property." In a nutshell, a non-title-holding spouse gets a share of marital property, but does not share in separate property (though there are many exceptions to this).

New York Domestic Relations Law section 236 defines "marital property" as "all property acquired by either or both spouses during the marriage and before the execution of a separation agreement or the commencement of a matrimonial action, regardless of the form in which title is held," except pursuant to the terms of a validly-drawn separation agreement, pre/post-nuptial agreement, or stipulation of settlement.

The same statute defines "separate property" to mean (1) property acquired before marriage or property acquired by bequest, devise, or descent, or gift from a party other than the spouse; (2) compensation for personal injuries; (3) property acquired in exchange for or the increase in value of separate property, except to the extent that such appreciation is due in part to the contributions or efforts of the other spouse; (4) property described as separate property by written agreement of the parties (as described above).

Thus, some cases are contested on whether a property of asset is "gifted" to 1 spouse by a relative during the marriage. The trial would then turn on what evidence there is that the gift was intended to only benefit the title-holding spouse, as opposed to benefitting the marriage as a whole.

****

A couple of other common misconceptions routinely "rear their ugly heads."

One is regarding child custody – many parents who have "sole custody" (see Chapter 8) think they can relocate without the permission of the non-custodial parent. They cannot not. Doing so puts them at substantial jeopardy the Judge will order them to return the child to New York pending trial – and if they've established residence and/or employment in the other state, they'd have to leave everything behind to come back to New York (or give up custody of their child).

Another is the concern of non-monied spouses that they can't afford a divorce lawyer, even if his/her spouse earns a lot of money.

In New York, the divorce law makes payment of counsel fees presumptive by the more-monied spouse to the less-monied spouse's attorney. This means if the case becomes contested, the party who doesn't earn all that much (if anything) can make an application to the Judge to force the other side to pay a portion of (or all of) the fees his/her own attorney would charge them.

At the uncontested stage, contribution towards the counsel fees of the less-monied spouse is subject to negotiation – there is no way to force this at the uncontested phase. I usually use the threat of counsel fees as a "carrot-and-stick" – either negotiate a fair settlement to my less-monied client, or else I will file a motion which will include a request for counsel fees. And in the greater-NYC area at least, such awards are anywhere from a few thousand dollars to as much as $10-25,000 (or more). If one is the more-monied spouse, this presumption creates a great incentive to make a "good offer" to the other side, lest one be settled with paying not only their own attorney, but the other side's attorney as well.

CHAPTER 4
DIVISION OF ASSETS IN A DIVORCE

New York is an equitable distribution state, which does not necessarily mean that assets are divided 50/50. There are a lot of nuances that come into play.

"Equitable" is just another word for fair. And there are numerous statutory factors a Judge will use to decide "what is fair" in any given case[13].

---

[13] The statutory factors are: (1) the income and property of each party at the time of marriage, and (2) the duration of the marriage and the age and health of both parties; (3) the need of a custodial parent to occupy or own the marital residence and to use or own its household effects; (4) the loss of inheritance and pension rights upon dissolution of the marriage as of the date of dissolution; (5) the loss of health

So, I'll give an example on retirement assets. There are a variety of ways we can divide retirement assets so the presumptive or general rule is that somebody will get 50% of the marital portion of the retirement asset. In other words, the amount which accrued to the account between the date of the marriage and the date of the commencement of the divorce proceeding is divided in half, and that's what you get.

That's a rather simplistic way of going about it - and there are many different ways parties can otherwise divide a retirement asset. That's why it benefits you to have an experienced divorce attorney representing you. If the

---

insurance benefits upon dissolution of the marriage; (6) any award of maintenance under subdivision six of this part; (7) any equitable claim to, interest in, or direct or indirect contribution made to the acquisition of such marital property by the party not having title, including joint efforts or expenditures and contributions and services as a spouse, parent, wage earner and homemaker, and to the career or career potential of the other party; (8) the liquid or non-liquid character of all marital property; (9) the probable future financial circumstances of each party; (10) the impossibility or difficulty of evaluating any component asset or any interest in a business, corporation or profession, and the economic desirability of retaining such asset or interest intact and free from any claim or interference by the other party; (11) the tax consequences to each party; (12) the wasteful dissipation of assets by either spouse; (13) any transfer or encumbrance made in contemplation of a matrimonial action without fair consideration; (14) any other factor which the court shall expressly find to be just and proper.

attorney is inexperienced, they'll likely only know that 1 simplistic way to divide the retirement asset - and they won't know the numerous other ways one can actually do it.

Another way one can divide a retirement asset is to do offsets of the two retirement portfolios. For example, one spouse has $200,000 in their retirement portfolio and the other spouse has $100,000 in their retirement portfolio. It doesn't necessarily make sense to have one spouse get half of $200,000 and the other spouse to get a half of $100,000. It actually makes better sense to just say that one spouse will get one half of the offset between the two retirement portfolios. That way, you don't need to have dueling qualified domestic relations orders to divide out these retirement assets.

Another way of deviating from the general rule is by moving the goal posts. In other words, the general rule is date of marriage to the date of commencement of the general divorce case, but that doesn't have to be the case. You can move the goalposts so the division is between the date of marriage and the date of physical separation. You can justify this by saying it wouldn't be fair to give the one spouse a share of the retirement assets which accrued after the parties stopped living together, as the other party cannot make a fair argument they made a "contribution" which allowed for the accrual of those retirement assets.

This discussion then goes to what is fair or equitable in any given case, and I've certainly been successful in my cases in negotiating that deviation from the general rule. Another option is to negotiate no distribution of retirements – a "he-keeps-his, she-keeps-hers" scenario.

****

There are many different types of assets - other than houses & condos - which are valued & divided in a divorce case.

A short list of the types of assets typically divided is as follows: real property, bank accounts, interests in businesses, bonuses, educational degrees, tax shelters, investments, jewelry, wedding gifts, personal property (including furniture), gifts exchanged between spouses, vested & unvested pension rights, vested or unvested, matured or unmatured pension rights, profit-sharing, retirement & savings plans, value of assets in a family asset protection trust, severance payment, value of "book business" of a broker, face value of insurance, frequent flyer miles and church (even if operated as non-profit).

Additionally, common forms of "separate property" are premarital property & assets, inherited property/assets, gifted property/assets (when clearly gifted to only 1 spouse) and personal injury compensation. The bottom line is that these are general rules & there are many exceptions made to the general rules. Each case is ultimately decided on its own merits and each situation brings to the table unique facts.

****

With the increasing cost of housing, many intact couples do not find they have a ton of money left over after paying their mortgage as well as their basic living expenses. When those same couples split up, however, they may be left with less money than is necessary to meet those expenses.

While the real estate market is not great right now (2017) for sellers, if the mortgage is otherwise eating you alive, you may have no choice but to sell. Couples often budget a mortgage factored on two incomes coming into 1 household. When the couple goes through a divorce, now they are left with trying to support 2 households - meaning 2 sets of utility bills as well as payment of the mortgage as well as payment of rent for the spouse who's moved out. It's not uncommon for this to leave the parties at the break-even point - or even leave them with less money than is needed to pay all their basic expenses. If this is the case, then the best option is to immediately put the house on the market & salvage what you can of the equity.

The other option - if one party wishes to keep the house but the parties cannot afford to fund 2 households - is for the party wishing to keep the house to get a co-signor on the mortgage. That way, the party giving up his/her rights can get a buy-out from the refinance & go on with his/her life. Making these decisions sooner rather than later in the divorce process will save on attorney's fees as well as preserve equity you've worked so hard to build up in the house.

Nevertheless, there are cases where the parties get married, but it's pretty much a rocky marriage throughout. Somebody lives downstairs and somebody lives upstairs, they don't joint ("co-mingle") bank accounts, they file separate taxes, and they pretty much live separate existences during their marriage. For the most part, they never formed an economic partnership in the first place.

In those rare instances, one can make the argument it would be unfair or inequitable for the other spouse who did not make any direct or indirect contribution (which allowed for the accrual of the marital asset(s)) to still get an equal share of those marital assets. Maybe instead of getting 50%, they should get a lower percentage. Perhaps they should only get 40% or 30%, or in rare cases nothing. I've certainly done cases where the courts have ruled after trial that the non-monied spouse will get nothing from the retirement assets because s/he never put in evidence of direct or indirect contribution to allow for the accrual of those assets.

****

The other issue to address is people who attempt to hide assets. I've been on both sides of the fence on this issue, where for example one spouse has significant assets in a U.S. bank or U.S. investment fund, and then transfers money into a foreign bank account. S/he doesn't disclose where the money went, and when they set forth their asset disclosure in their "net worth statement," they don't list that money. So, a lot of times, the opposing spouse will ask where that money went. The spouse will just shrug their shoulders and say, "I don't know. It must've gotten spent."

At that point, there is the issue of trying to trace the money and find out where exactly it went. In many instances, I advise clients to hire a forensic accountant. There are practical reasons for doing this. A forensic accountant is going to charge far less to review financial accounts than an attorney will charge. Good divorce attorneys generally charge between $400 and $500 an hour (or more) in Westchester and New York City. Forensic accountants, on the other hand, may only charge $250 to $300 an hour for their services. Moreover, a forensic accountant is going to know exactly what they are looking for because that's pretty much all they do.

They are going to review those financial accounts much more efficiently and cost effectively than an attorney would. Furthermore, a forensic accountant can actually testify to the court, whereas an attorney cannot. So, in situations where there is an allegation of hidden or secreted assets, I tell a potential client to hire a forensic accountant and have that analysis done sooner rather than later. Those issues are going to come up in settlement negotiations, and it's better to have that analysis ready to show to the judge or the referee in the settlement negotiations. Ironically, the sooner you prepare for trial, the better prepared you will be to negotiate a fair settlement.

The bottom line is there are a variety of ways one can divide assets in a divorce case - it's rarely as easy as "he gets half & she gets half & we're done."

****

Asset Protection in a Divorce

Before a divorce is filed, there are no restraints as far as what a spouse can legally do in terms of asset protection.

As such, the critical date is the divorce filing date. In New York, we have automatic orders that restrain a party presumptively from moving assets after a divorce is filed. So a lot of times – especially when it comes to financial accounts and bank accounts - I'll tell a client they may withdraw half, because s/he is entitled to half. You shouldn't take more than half because that's not fair, and it's not right.

I will never tell a client to just raid a joint account; I don't do that in good conscience. I'm simply not that kind of an attorney. Quite frankly, if a client came to me and told me they'd done that, I'd advise them to give the spouse back their one half. I always want to look like the good guy to the judge. I don't want to look like the bad guy to the judge, and I don't want my client to look like the bad guy either.

Selling property - even if it is in joint names - is absolutely permissible before a divorce is filed, so long as you have consent from the spouse who is going to have to sign off on the deed transfer. That's certainly permissible and people oftentimes do that where there is no dispute and they need the money to fund the divorce litigation.

Likewise, if the property is in the name of one spouse or the other, it's still permissible before the divorce is filed. After the divorce is filed, there has to be consent. So, either the other spouse will consent to the transfer of the property, or you have to get court permission.

Another thing that comes about is needed money to fund the litigation. The automatic orders definitely permit you to withdrawal money for reasonable attorney's fees from mere financial accounts throughout the divorce case.

Furthermore, mere financial accounts such as bank accounts, stocks, bonds, mutual funds, or similar accounts would *not* be classified as a retirement account. However, if you are purporting to take money out of a retirement account (e.g., pensions, 401(k)s, IRAs) once a divorce has already been filed, you need the express permission of your spouse or you need court permission.

If someone comes to me in a situation where divorce has not yet been filed, and if they even remotely think that it's going to be contested, I tell them if they don't have the $10,000 they'll need in order to do a contested divorce case, they should take it of their retirement account now. After a divorce is filed, you are going to have a problem because your spouse may or may not consent to you doing that, and then you are going to have to file a motion which is going to cost you several hundred dollars.

I have one case pending right now in which that exact scenario is playing out. The husband, who I am representing, thought his case was going to be an uncontested case, so he cobbled the money together to pay me the uncontested fee. Then, the case turned contested and I told him pursuant to your contract, you owe more money to me now because it's a contested case. He didn't have it - he said it was tied up in his 401(k). I had to tell him that since there is a divorce pending, I need consent from your spouse to access that 401(k). So, I went to her attorney and I said, "Look, we are willing to do a stipulation where it says my client can borrow from his retirement, but it will only be considered borrowing against his share of his retirement." Therefore, it completely protects the other spouse because it will not be considered as money coming out of her share or her potential share of his retirement.

Without providing a reason, the wife's attorney told me he was not willing to sign that stipulation. I tried to negotiate a further settlement, stating the situation was unreasonable. It's going to unnecessarily cause motion practice, and a judge is not going to be happy with me having to file a motion on this issue. I tried every angle I could to pry that consent out of the attorney, and the attorney still said no. So now, at a several hundred-dollar cost to my client, I had to go ahead and file the motion and hope the it will give that permission to him. If the judge does not give that permission and he cannot otherwise charge that money on his credit card, he may be left without a divorce attorney. All of this happened because he didn't consider a contested case to be a possibility at the outset of the divorce case.

****

Protection from Spouse's Debt

How someone can go about protecting themselves from their spouse's debt involves looking at how the debt arose.

Oftentimes, I've faced cases in which there is credit card debt that is in joint name. You'll have debt that's in one name or the other, and then it's a matter of seeing if that's all marital debt, or if some of it is separate debt. If there is an allegation that some of it is separate debt, then we have a look at the actual credit card statements themselves and examine what charges the particular party claims belong to other spouse's separate debt. So, separate debt means that even though two people accrued debt during that marriage, it was for their own separate purposes. For example, somebody goes to Sachs 5th avenue and puts $5000 worth of clothes on the credit card. Clearly, that was for their separate purposes, and they'll presumably be keeping those clothes even in the event of a divorce case. Likewise, if they went to the container store and bought several thousand dollars' worth of furniture and containers for the marital residence, and that spouse will continue to reside in that marital residence and therefore have the benefit of those belongings, then that debt should be considered their own separate debt.

If I have a client that makes that allegation, I first obtain the credit card statements going back three years or more. Then I have the clients actually sit down and go over what they believe to be separate debt. Sometimes that requires a forensic accountant, and sometimes the charges on the credit card statements are not all that clear. In that case, we have to subpoena the actual receipts themselves from the stores or restaurants in order to determine what exactly was purchased.

In regards to mortgage debt, if the mortgage was accrued during the marriage itself, it's presumptively marital, so oftentimes there is no dispute along those lines. However, there could be disputes arising from separate property contributions, whether those are premarital funds used as a down payment on the mortgage, or a gift from a relative that one spouse wants to allege was given specifically to them and not to benefit the marriage itself.

The other consideration is whether or not there is debt wrapped up in utility bills. Oftentimes, the spouse who remains in the house doesn't have the income to support two different houses, and the utility bills that are connected to the house fall by the way side. Then the debate becomes who pays what.

CHAPTER 5
ALIMONY OR SPOUSAL SUPPORT – AN OVERVIEW

Maintenance (other states use the term "alimony") is determined by a number of issues relating to a marriage. It may be temporary or permanent.

Although it is not a given right to either spouse, the courts will generally order a certain amount of spousal support based on the following factors (this is a non-exhaustive list): duration of the marriage, income of both spouses, age of both spouses, health/special needs of either spouse, circumstances surrounding spousal support are unique to each couple, and therefore the court uses its discretion when determining maintenance orders.

In most cases, attorneys' fees for matters surrounding maintenance are paid for by the spouse with the higher income. Indeed, in 2010, New York passed statutes making interim maintenance & counsel fees presumptively awarded on all cases involving a higher-earning spouse versus a lower-earning spouse.

Additionally, as with child support orders, a maintenance order may be modified if the court can be shown there has been a substantial change of circumstances in the life of either party involved (though if there was a valid written agreement such as a "stipulation of settlement" or "separation agreement," the standard to modify may be "unanticipated change of circumstances").

As of 2010, New York has presumptive calculations to arrive at what the "general rule" is for maintenance between two parties. This means that they start with the parties' incomes and use two sets of formulae that the court calculates. One calculation is to determine whether the payer is going to be paying child support or is going to be the recipient of child support. If they are going to be the payer, then it's 20% of the payer's income minus 25% of the payee's income. If it's the recipient, then it's 30% of the payer's income minus 20% of the payee's income. The court also compares that to 40% of combined income, minus the payee's income. Whichever comes out less is the presumptive amount of maintenance. So, it's a rather convoluted formula which is why I'll return to the calculator to do that calculation.

The other factor is that the presumptive amount only goes up to a combined income of $178,000[14]. That's at least a presumptive cap currently in effect, though that cap is adjusted bi-annually pursuant to the consumer price index, and it goes up by a few thousand dollars every other two years. So that will result in the presumptive amount of maintenance. Then, there are various factors that the court will consider in deviating from that presumptive amount or interim amounts of maintenance. In other words, while the divorce is pending, there are 13 statutory factors that the court will consider in the final award, although the statute characterizes that as a post-divorce award. There are 15

---

[14] This "cap" increases once every 2 years based on the consumer price index. This is the "cap" amount as of the publishing of this book.

statutory factors that the court will consider in arriving at the proper amount or deviating from the presumptive amounts. That's the basic way that maintenance is calculated.

If you're a high-wage earner, and your spouse earns little or nothing, then you face the prospect of paying spousal maintenance (i.e., alimony).

If you face the prospect of paying maintenance, one thing you should do is document to your spouse that you want him/her to find employment - or if they are working, to find a better job or go back to school. You should do everything in your power to encourage his/her job efforts. Send him/her job listings, for instance. If s/he isn't working due to child care, offer to have the child(ren) stay with a relative or find daycare. Does your spouse have employable skills or work history & is simply squandering them? Consider hiring a headhunter or employability expert to assist in the process.

There are 15 factors considered in arriving at the "proper" amount of maintenance[15]. Was this a short-term

---

[15] (1)The age and health of the parties; (2) The present or future earning capacity of the parties, including a history of limited participation in the workforce; (3) The need of one party to incur

marriage (less than 10 years)? Do you have a high amount of marital debt (indicative of living above your means during the marriage)? Does your spouse have a college or graduate degree which may create high earning potential? Was the degree earned during the marriage? Is your spouse likely to get a relatively high distribution of assets from the marriage? Does your spouse own any separate

---

education or training expenses; (4)The termination of a child support award before the termination of the maintenance award when the calculation of maintenance was based upon child support being awarded which resulted in a maintenance award lower than it would have been had child support not been awarded; (5) The wasteful dissipation of marital property, including transfers or encumbrances made in contemplation of a matrimonial action without fair consideration; (6) The existence and duration of a pre-marital joint household or a pre-divorce separate household; (7) Acts by one party against another that have inhibited or continue to inhibit a party's earning capacity or ability to obtain meaningful employment. Such acts include but are not limited to acts of domestic violence as provided in section four hundred fifty-nine-a of the social services law; (8) The availability and cost of medical insurance for the parties; (9)The care of children or stepchildren, disabled adult children or stepchildren, elderly parents or in-laws provided during the marriage that inhibits a party's earning capacity; (10) The tax consequences to each party; (11) The standard of living of the parties established during the marriage; (12) The reduced or lost earning capacity of the payee as a result of having foregone or delayed education, training, employment or career opportunities during the marriage; (13) The equitable distribution of marital property and the income or imputed income on the assets so distributed; (14) The contributions and services of the payee as a spouse, parent, wage earner and homemaker and to the career or career potential of the other party; and (15) Any other factor which the court shall expressly find to be just and proper.

property (or have any separate assets)? Are you covering your spouse on your health insurance (and is there an additional amount you pay to cover him/her)? All of these are common factors considered in reducing or eliminating the potential for the Court to award maintenance.

****

Can Spousal Maintenance Awards Be Modified?

The modification will depend on whether or not there is a settlement agreement in place. If there is a settlement agreement in place, it is essential to have a provision saying that the maintenance amount can be adjusted on a normal substantial change of circumstance. A substantial change of circumstance is such that either side's income goes up or down by 50% or more. This could be caused by the loss of employment, a substantial change in expenses, or something else along those lines. However, if the settlement agreement is silent on how maintenance can be adjusted over time, then the court borrows from regular contract law and says that the only way you can change maintenance is on a standard of unanticipated change of circumstances. That makes it extremely hard to change a maintenance amount, because the other side can say that you signed this contract agreeing to this amount, and perhaps I gave up other claims in the divorce case in exchange for this amount. Now that you are changing that amount, it wouldn't be fair for me to have given up all those other things in the divorce case, or to have paid more for those things if I'd known my maintenance would be adjusted. That's why the courts generally make it pretty hard to change maintenance if you do so pursuant to a settlement agreement that does not otherwise provide for a lower basis to change the amount.

Chapter 6
CHILD SUPPORT – HOW IT WORKS IN NEW YORK

In New York, the process of child support determination is similar to the process of alimony determination.

The child support statute is set up to technically look at both parties' incomes, and there are presumptive calculations of support. There was a seminar that I went to years ago that ran varied calculations either way, and it really doesn't matter how you do the calculations. It works out the same as if you simply went straight to the non-custodial parent's income and just applied the statutory formula to that income.

So, the statutory percentages are 17% of adjusted gross income for one child, 25% for two children, 29% for three children, 31% for four children, and 35% for five or more children. This calculation arrives at the presumptive amount. Obviously, there are varying factors in deviating from the presumptive amount. Nevertheless, one can simply compare the noncustodial parent's income to the child support percentage to know what the "general rule" is[16].

Many non-custodial parents think child support is just calculated on his/her base salary. Think again! All income counts, so this will include overtime or income from a 2d job. As such, if the custodial parent threatens to sue for child support, you may wish to consider cutting back on overtime, or giving up that 2d job - or else you may be stuck with having to keep earning that income whether you like it or not.

Some people don't realize if they have rental income, dividend income, or income from investments

---

[16] https://www.childsupport.ny.gov/dcse/pdfs/CSSA.pdf.

that it counts as income for child support purposes as well. Additionally, if you receive a tax refund, then guess what? That's income as well. The good rule of thumb to use is: any money coming into your wallet is probably going to be considered income for child support purposes. Be forewarned!

There are also some other factors the court considers: day care expenses, medical/dental insurance costs and educational expenses - if the custodial parent incurs these expenses and they are unreimbursed, the non-custodial parent may be obligated to pay a portion of these expenses in addition to payment of the "basic child support" as explained above[17].

---

[17] The total factors are: (1) The financial resources of the custodial and non-custodial parent, and those of the child; (2) The physical and emotional health of the child and his/her special needs and aptitudes; (3) The standard of living the child would have enjoyed had the marriage or household not been dissolved; (4) The tax consequences to the parties; (5) The non-monetary contributions that the parents will make toward the care and well-being of the child; (6) The educational needs of either parent; (7) A determination that the gross income of one parent is substantially less than the other parent's gross income; (8) The needs of the children of the non-custodial parent for whom the non-custodial parent is providing support who are not subject to the instant action and whose support has not been deducted from income pursuant to subclause (D) of clause (vii) of subparagraph five of paragraph (b) of this subdivision, and the financial resources of

Common ways one can deviate from the presumptive amount is if their combined parental income exceeds the statutory cap of $143,000. Again, that "cap" amount is adjusted biannually pursuant to the consumer price index. Another common way of deviating is if one parent has some type of unusual living expense, especially for the non-custodial parent. If they are looking at the deviation, then that means an expense that the normal average person does not have. They will not get a deviation if, for example, a person just has high housing expenses, high food bills, or high utility bills. This is because those categories are expenses that everyone has. In order to get a deviation, they have to provide proof of an unusual expense, such as a high medical

---

any person obligated to support such children, provided, however, that this factor may apply only if the resources available to support such children are less than the resources available to support the children who are subject to the instant action; (9) Provided that the child is not on public assistance (i) extraordinary expenses incurred by the non-custodial parent in exercising visitation, or (ii) expenses incurred by the non-custodial parent in extended visitation provided that the custodial parent's expenses are substantially reduced as a result thereof; and (10) Any other factors the court determines are relevant in each case, the court shall order the non-custodial parent to pay his or her pro rata share of the basic child support obligation, and may order the non-custodial parent to pay an amount pursuant to paragraph (e) of this subdivision.

cost or a medical condition for which they have a lot of unreimbursed medical expenses.

I've also been successful in getting deviations based on a high amount of debt, particularly student loan debt that automatically comes out of someone's income and leaves them with less disposable income than the average person. The other common way you can get a deviation is if you have significant access time with a child. So, that doesn't necessarily mean you pay no child support, but if you have the child in your care for approximately 40% or 50% of the time, you can at least make the argument to the magistrate that they could consider the expenses that you have to lay out while the child is at your house in justifying a deviation from what guideline support often is.

The standard visitation for non-custodial parents is alternate weekends. So, if that's all that a non-custodial parent has, they are less likely to be successful on that deviation argument from child support.

Some people share custody of their child - which means exactly 50%-50% in each household. The issue then becomes whether child support is paid at all - and if so, how much.

The first analysis is whether the shared custody arrangement is pursuant to court order, or just by a mutual, informal agreement. If it's pursuant to court order, then you can skip to the 2d section below. If it's pursuant to informal agreement, then you're best advised to start keeping track of the days (& even hours of those days) the child is with you. Reason being: if there's a dispute later on about whether you do indeed shared custody, then at least you have something in writing to corroborate same. You should also begin confirming the days you'll have the child with the other parent in writing. As an example, you can send a calendar to the other parent for the next month marking off "M" or "F" on the days to designate which days the child will be with you versus the other parent. In the end, you're best advised to file a petition for shared custody & get the arrangement confirmed via court order.

The prevailing law - however incorrect - holds that in a shared custody situation the parent who makes more is automatically deemed the noncustodial parent & is thus potentially liable for the full guidelines amount (i.e., 17%

for 1 child, 25% for 2, etc.). That said, many courts deviate from the presumptive calculation in a shared custody situation & do an off-set: first, then calculate support as if the father is paying the mother support. Then they calculate as if the mother pays the father support. The difference between the two calculations would therefore be the only money changing hands.

If the other parent threatens to sue you for child support & you're already supporting another child, then the very first thing you should do - if you do NOT already have a child support order for that 1st child - is to have a written agreement drawn between you & the mother of that 1st child. The agreement should be drafted by a capable child support lawyer, as there's particular language which should go in there so it's valid.

You are best advised to then file a petition in Family Court & get a Support Magistrate to issue a court order based on the agreement. Then if the mother of the 2d child files a petition for a support order, you can produce a copy of that agreement and/or order, along with proof of payment, and you should receive a credit for supporting that 1st child.

Additionally, in 2010, New York law amended its child support guidelines to include an automatic modification of child support once every three years. This means that if your child support order is up for a review, you may simply file a petition at the 3-year mark & have the Court re-calculate support based on current incomes. Moreover, if you or your child's parent has undergone a substantial change in circumstances, warranting a modification, the court can also assess your situation to determine if a modification is necessary.

A guy came in to see me saying the mother of his child was suing him for 50% of college expenses. He said he was already paying basic support & simply didn't have any money left. I reviewed his settlement agreement - it clearly said he was to pay for college. Bottom line: he was screwed! Lesson learned: save for college when they're young!

Child Support in New York generally continues until age 21 & thus includes payment towards college expenses. If the parent did not start a 529 plan early on, then s/he will still generally be liable for their share of college expenses - whether they can afford it or not. As such, if you have a child in grade school, it's best to start a 529 plan now or else set yourself up to get screwed later (or hope they attend public school). Support Magistrates will most likely impose the expense of college on the non-custodial parent even when he/she is already paying basic child support. Thus, it's a double-whammy: If you're making $50,000/year, you could already be paying $150 per week in basic support - and then on top of that you could be $100 or more per week towards college expenses. Lesson: save now or hurt later!

Chapter 7
CHILD CUSTODY, VISITATION & FAMILY OFFENSE ISSUES

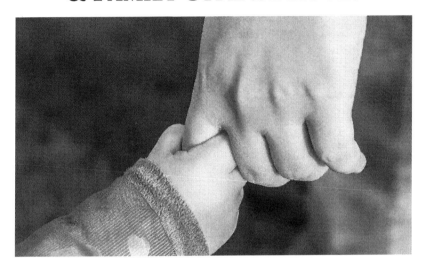

Oftentimes, issues surrounding custody of a child, visitation and/or domestic violence are the "meat" of a divorce case – the ones causing the most litigation as well as the most emotion.

In New York, custody of children can be determined in a number of ways:

1. JOINT CUSTODY: In a joint custody situation, both parents have the legal authority to make major life decisions on behalf of their child concerning issues like religion, education or health care. Sometimes they agree to have "equal decision-making" which means they must reach agreement on all major decisions, or else the decision would be submitted to

a mediator or Judge to decide. In other agreements, the primary custodial parent gets final decision-making after full consultation with the non-custodial parent. Joint Custody in New York is often reached via agreement but rarely imposed upon the parents by the Judge.

2. SOLE CUSTODY: When a parent is given sole custody, the child will physically live with him or her, and he or she will have the ultimate authority to make every day and major life decisions for the child.

3. SHARED CUSTODY: When parents share custody, they generally split their access to the child 50/50. A shared custody situation is very rare.

4. SPLIT CUSTODY: This is a situation in which at least 1 child lives with one parent, and at least 1 child lives with the other parent. Negotiating a custody plan can be complex. It is important to remember that the court ultimately looks at what is in the best interests of the child. For fathers, this means that if you and your child's mother separate, it is important to remain in the child's life as much as possible. Both parents -- custodial or noncustodial -- should keep as much physical evidence as possible that may strengthen their case.

The overall standard is the "best interests of the child." However, within that standard the court considers "the totality of the circumstances." That said, there are a number of other specific factors the court considers when awarding custody as between two biological parents.

The Judge will generally consider the stability of the child's current arrangement, each parent's home environment and financial ability to meet the child's needs, any arrangements to care for the child when the parent is unavailable, who has been the primary caretaker for the child in the years (or months) leading up to the custody filing, any drug/alcohol use by either parent, the mental & physical health of the parties, adverse sexual misconduct of either parent, domestic violence, as well as the child's preferences.

The court will also assess each parent's willingness to foster a relationship between the other parent and the child, any denial of access to the child, as well as any abuse or neglect of the child. Finally, the Judge will assess the parties conduct as the case is proceeding, including conduct both in and out of the courtroom.

I must first caution - no matter how tense the situation may be around the house – you should *generally* not move out of the house & leave the kids with the other parent. This will automatically put you behind the 8-ball in winning custody.

Additionally, if you haven't been already, take an active part in EVERYTHING the children are involved in.

Make sure his/her teachers, doctors, extracurricular activity instructors, etc. know you by your first name.

If you presently work long hours, reduce them immediately - spend the extra time with your kids. Take them fun places & buy them nice gifts - though caution must be used not to over-do it as otherwise it would look like you're trying the bribe them.

Keep a written diary of any important conversations or interactions with the other parent (a "he-said-she-said" log). Refrain from posting negative content about the other parent on social media as this is potentially discoverable - if you have something to say to a friend/family member, say it in person. Refrain from cursing or denigrating the other parent, especially in writing (I don't know how many cases I have in which one side curses or denigrates the other via text and/or e-mail).

****

Many people contemplate divorce, but are still living in the same household with their minor children. The question then becomes - how is custody handled?

One way to resolve the issue is for the parties to agree on which parent may have custody, and then allow him/her to move out with the children while the case is pending. It's best that each party have a lawyer and an interim stipulation be drawn up to this effect.

If there's no agreement, then neither parent should move out just yet. Instead, if there's either domestic violence present or same is imminent, then an application for exclusive occupancy and temporary custody should be filed. If that's not the case, then you will then just need to go through the process of a contested custody case. You should both have lawyers who have good experience handling such cases. Generally, the Court will also assign an Attorney to represent the children - and generally will order (though not always) a forensic psychological evaluation on the custody issue.

****

I face many situations in which a mother has voluntarily given custody of her children over to the father. Many times, this happens because the mother wants to go back to school to obtain a degree, or because the mother's house is cramped & the father just moved into a new, larger space.

Regardless, the mother feels in doing so that the arrangement will just be "temporary." Sometimes the father even expressly states, "I won't give you any problems in giving you back the kids when you finish school."

If only everything were just that simple. When a Child Custody lawyer must get involved, it's because the situation has changed, but now the father will not give the kids back. The mother has no proof of their informal arrangement and therefore must satisfy a high legal burden in order to get an order from a Judge switching custody. What to do?

First, mothers in this situation should get the temporary nature of the arrangement captured in writing, preferably in a custody order which provides that mother may petition for custody again when her circumstances change (while stating in the order itself what exact circumstances may create the change).

Second, it's preferable to have the father sign a notarized letter, affidavit or stipulation stating his intentions of giving the children back upon, for example, mother finishing school.

Finally, any conversations of significance between father & mother should be captured in writing, which usually takes the form of a confirmatory e-mail.

While these steps won't guarantee a mother gets custody back, they'll put her in a much better position that doing nothing at all & assuming "everything will fall into place."

****

Family Offense & Domestic Violence

Many people are unaware that domestic violence is NOT limited to disputes among married persons. Domestic violence can also occur between family members or intimate partners. But increasingly, domestic violence issues are intertwined in divorce cases.

In New York, the allegations may include (this is a non-exhaustive list): disorderly conduct, criminal mischief, assault, harassment, menacing and stalking.

New York law was recently amended to allow for restraining orders or orders of protection to anyone who is involved in an intimate relationship (generally termed "boyfriend" or "girlfriend" relationships). This change affords victims extra security when it comes to domestic violence.

Proof that there's been an act of domestic violence is the only statutory factor currently considered by the court's as specifically bearing on a parent's fitness to have custody of a minor child (within contested custody litigation).

If you feel you may have been a victim of domestic violence, it is generally advised (at the least) that you consult with your attorney on the issue – if not file for an order of protection. Depending on the circumstances, you may also wish to call the police or contact an agency which handles domestic violence matters.

Finally, there are many resources online one can turn to for assistance – a good start is the court's website: http://www.nycourts.gov/topics/domesticViolence.shtml.

Chapter 8
QUALITIES TO LOOK FOR
IN A FAMILY LAW ATTORNEY

Increasingly people are considering the price of hiring a family law attorney. No one wants to spend more than they have to, and certainly price is one practical consideration people have.

Even in the greater New York city area, you can easily find divorce attorneys who will only charge you a few hundred dollars up-front. You'll also find middle of the road divorce attorneys who will charge anything from a few thousand to anywhere from $5000 to $10,000. And you can find elite divorce attorneys that will charge somewhere in the range of $10,000 to $25,000 or more up-front - all before they even look at you. Suffice it to say, there are a lot of reasons which factor into *why* attorneys charge different amounts.

Going to see a lawyer is very dissimilar to going to see a doctor - because when you go to see a doctor, you don't ask how many years they've been out of medical school, what school they attended, what grades they received, or what type of experience they have. No one grills his/her doctor on such factors - but they *absolutely should* interview their prospective attorney like that. Even if you don't necessarily have the confidence to ask those questions at a one-on-one consultation, you should nevertheless be able to glean the information you need right from the attorney's website[18]. You should feel free to email the attorney and ask the questions you need in order to effectively assess their qualifications and experience.

---

[18] Steer clear of attorneys who fail to put the basic of their qualifications on their websites. I was just retained on a divorce case & as I usually do, I checked out the opposing attorney's site. It said nothing at all about how long the attorney had been in practice. Why is she ducking that basic fact? As a prospective customer, one should worry if his/her attorney feels they have something to hide *before you even hire them.*

One factor to look at is their experience. Some attorneys are fresh out of law school, while some attorneys have 10 or 20 years of experience – still others have 30 or more years of experience. And experience is certainly one factor you should consider. However, you shouldn't conclude that merely because one attorney has 30 years of experience and another has only 10 or 20 years of experience, presumptively the one with 30 years of experience is better. You have to dig deeper and determine *the nature* of the experience.

For instance, if an attorney has 30 years of experience, but only 10% of his/her practice covers divorce law, you may want to seek an attorney with more experience in dealing specifically with divorce cases.

Even if the attorney with 30 years' experience *claims* that 50% of his/her practice covers divorce law, you should ask *for how long* that has been the case. Maybe this has only been the case since the real estate bubble burst (back in 2007 or 2008). If this is the case, then only over the last 10 years or so has 50% or more of their practice been divorce law. If an attorney has 20 years of experience, but close to 100% of their practice is divorce law *and that has been the case throughout all*

20 years of practice, then that attorney is going to be a better qualified (all else being equal) to take your case.

The other question to ask your prospective attorney is how many cases they generally handle at one time. The reason this is relevant is because there have been studies that say it is arguably malpractice for a typical family law attorney in New York to do more than about 70 cases at a time. In fact, there was a deposition testimony given in a case called *Nicholson vs. Scopetta*. The testimony was given by two of the heads of Attorneys for Children panels here in New York City. They gave sworn testimony saying that no family law practitioner should have anything more than approximately 50 to 70 cases.

Despite this, you will absolutely find family law attorneys who have anywhere from 80 to 150 cases they are handling at a time. The problem is if you are handling many more cases than the research says can be handled responsibly, one of two things are invariably occurring: either that attorney is literally working 24 hours a day, seven days a week, and burning themselves out, or they are committing varied forms of malpractice on at least some of the cases. Malpractice oftentimes comes in through sheer neglect of cases. I often refer to those firms as "divorce mills," because you'll oftentimes see groupings of these law firms in and around the courthouses. Sometimes they will even have neon signs in their windows that read, "Divorce Attorney!"

A lot of times, people who don't have a lot of money will be desperate and will pay a few hundred dollars to these firms to process their divorce cases. As a practical matter, if you don't have a lot of money to afford a divorce attorney, then it's an unfortunate but practical consideration you have to make. In that case, price will be your overriding factor in who you hire.

For most other people who make a halfway decent income, knowing how many cases your attorney is handling at any given time is absolutely a question that you should ask. Some divorce attorneys serve as public defenders - which is a noble profession. In fact, I am on the Attorneys for Children panel in Westchester County. Historically, I've occasionally accepted adult assignments through the courts as well, and people should do that. That's giving back to the community and to the less fortunate.

However, if you have decent income, and you are considering hiring an attorney, do you want to hire an attorney who has 100 public defender cases on their docket, and is literally doing three, four, or five cases a day? Do you want an attorney who is running around like a chicken with their head cut off, and can't even remember their client's names? Resist the temptation to allow price to be your guide when selecting your divorce attorney!

I was once hired by a client who had a decent income working for the NYPD. She was earning approximately $100,000 a year, and she hired me after having hired one of my competitors here in the Bronx. He is relatively notorious for having a caseload of between 100 and 150 cases. He is a typical mill attorney. This client had a relatively simple child support case, with no complicating factors. On the very first court date, her attorney showed up no less than four hours late for the court case, and never called her or the court to say that he was running late. When he finally showed up, he didn't know who she was. He had to call out in the waiting area, blurting her name out so that everyone could hear it. Then he went up to her and basically shrugged his shoulders. He never apologized, he went into court and the judge said, "Too late, I'm not doing your case." The case was adjourned for three months.

To make matters worse, this client was penalized further when the Magistrate refused to set a temporary order of support. So my client, who was struggling financially, went without support for three months while awaiting her next court date. Suffice it to say, she learned the hard way that an important question to ask your prospective family law attorney is how many cases they will be handling at any one time. She went in with the misconception that she could hire any family law attorney, and she thought she was getting a really good deal. So, for someone who earns decent money, price should not be your number one consideration in hiring an attorney. Instead, you should focus on quality.

The father in that same case chose to hire an attorney who is also on the public defender panel and carries a caseload of between 100 to 150 cases. That attorney treated the case the same way. So, on each court date we had, he called out the client's name in the waiting area because he had no idea of who he was. Each time the case was on, the guy would always say he was in a rush. On one of the dates, he had a trial and forgot to tell his own client he couldn't appear that day. When I expressed to him it was really not professional to accept a private retainer on a day he had multiple other cases on, he basically just shrugged his shoulders and walked away. The case got adjourned that day to the chagrin of his own client.

So, what consequences did it have for his client on that case? When we went to resolve the case, his attorney came up to me and wanted to negotiate a settlement. I looked him in the eye and told him I wasn't willing to negotiate a single thing because of the way he had conducted himself on the case. He walked away on multiple court dates, causing my client financial strain. Instead of knowing the law well enough and really having researched this particular case in order to negotiate a fair settlement, he literally shrugged his shoulders, went back to his client and said, "Oh well! They don't want to negotiate, so I guess we're stuck with the guidelines for child support." He then turned away, went into the courtroom, and waited for the case to be called.

There is no doubt that through the multiple adjournments, this guy probably paid his attorney a couple of thousand dollars to do this case. This attorney ended up being nothing better than a warm body in the seat next to him. That client made approximately $150,000 a year and certainly could have hired a far better attorney to represent him, but he mistakenly used price as the number one consideration in whom to hire. Now he's stuck with a much higher child support amount for the life of the case because he chose to save a couple of hundred dollars on his attorney.

****

Red Flags Associated With Divorce Attorneys

I'm a big believer in a jack of all trades and master of none. So, you'll definitely find attorneys out there who have signs or ads saying they do divorce law, bankruptcy, real estate, slip and falls, etc. They will pretty much take any case which comes along.

Think about it this way: if you have a serious heart problem, would you just go into a general practitioner, or would you go to a cardiac specialist? Most people would say they want to see a cardiac specialist in that instance, *because they want to live*. It's the same thing with the law.

If you go into a general practitioner who practices several different areas of law, they are not a specialist, and they are dividing out their experience into all those areas of law. So, when it comes time for the nuances, to negotiate successful settlements or even to do a divorce trial, they are not going to know how to handle those nuances as well as a specialist would.

I had a potential client that came into my office who had gone to a general practitioner. The general practitioner had told her she would not qualify for maintenance if she was not a housewife. I found this advice so far removed from the truth it was outright deceiving, yet the people who walk into that attorney's office don't know any better if they don't shop around or go to a specialist. I already went into how New York has maintenance guidelines and a maintenance calculator to arrive at the proper amount - in no way, shape or form is there a requirement that the prospective recipient be a housewife in order to get maintenance.

The same general practitioner said to the same potential client that if she had child custody or child support issues, she should go to Family Court and file there first - and only then should she come back and do the divorce case. Sometimes that's good advice, but in her case it was horrible advice. This is because of the fact that she and her spouse were currently living together. If she had tried to file her child custody or support case in family court, most likely they would have rejected it[19] and she would have wasted time. Moreover, if she had retained this attorney to do this family court case, she would have wasted that money.

That's all the more reason to really make sure that you have a specialist. If you have an important custody or visitation issue, child support issue and/or you have a high amount of property or finances at stake in your divorce case, you really want somebody that is well experienced in your particular area of law.

****

Attorneys with Their Own Agendas

In addition to the above, I often tell people that I tend to take anyone who has a good case and is willing to pay my

---

[19] Usually Family Court will not accept custody, visitation or child support filings involving married parties who still reside together – instead they usually advise them to file for divorce.

fee - without me having an agenda. You will definitely find some family law attorneys who say they're a "father's rights attorney," or a "mother's rights attorney," or an advocate on behalf of domestic violence victims, and so on. The problem is that the attorney has a clear agenda, and they are invariably imposing their own values or beliefs on your case irrespective of whether that's right for your case.

For example, I had an attorney on a case that was a mother's rights advocate. She mostly represented females. She incorrectly advised her client by telling her maintenance (otherwise known as alimony) is "an entitlement of women." Even though this woman had teaching credentials and she could go back into the workforce and be a teacher earning $60,000, $70,000 or $80,000 a year, this attorney actually advised her not to look for a job. Instead, she advised her to stay at home and ask for maintenance from her husband, because that's "her entitlement as a woman." Not only is this notion offensive to women - to treat them like that and to assume it's their proper role to essentially be a housewife instead of someone out working in the workforce - but she is also clearly imposing her own personal beliefs and values on her client, which is equally wrong.

You therefore want to ask your potential attorney if they represent more women or men, or if it's pretty much equal. You should ask your potential attorney if they have any agendas they are trying to pursue in terms of representing clients.

****

Finally, another assessment in retaining a good attorney to ask is what the objective criteria are which support hiring that attorney. For instance, are they a former prosecutor? If so, that's unparalleled experience, especially in terms of trial experience. The other objective criteria to look at are their AVVO ratings. Are they listed as a Super Lawyer by Thompson Reuters? Do they have an AV rating from Martindale Hubbell? What are their client reviews?

Moreover, you can go on various websites such as AVVO and Google and look at their client reviews. A good attorney is no doubt going to have a few negative reviews. If you go on Amazon and look at the best products out there, somebody is going to be displeased with that product. But if you go and look at a particular, very popular product on Amazon, you might see a hundred reviews. If only five of them are negative, that should not dissuade you from buying that product, because that product has a 95% approval rating. Likewise, when you go on and look at a lawyer, if they have 100 reviews and 95% of them are positive, then that's a good attorney. You want to hire that attorney. If an attorney has no reviews at all, then you can't assess whether their clients even like them, and that should be a factor. If they only have 10 or 20 reviews and a disproportionate share are negative, then that should also be a consideration that you make.

A final note about fake accolades or fake reviews. There are some websites cropping up which "sell accolades" to attorneys which make them appear good, but there's no verification process. Thus, you may see an attorney with a badge on their website saying they're a "TOP DIVORCE ATTORNEY" or in the "Top 20% of Divorce Attorneys." Be wary of such fake accolades.

How do you know? If an accolade is connected to an organization, any good organization is going to be connected to a major legal publishing (Thompson Reuters, American Law Media, Martindale Hubbell), etc.), a bar Association, or be connected to an independent company or lawyers' committee which has an extensive website promoting what it does, how many lawyers are associated with it, whether it's bar approved, etc. Don't hesitate to ask that attorney if s/he advertises that they're a "Top 10% attorney" how the organization who awarded the accolade arrived at that determination. If they don't know (or can quickly point you to information allowing you to verify for yourself), then walk out.

Fake reviews – they happen, and there's little way a consumer can verify the real ones from the fake ones. Just be wary if an attorney has all positive reviews, or an attorney has hundreds of reviews while other competitors have 10-20. S/he may be paying for their reviews – thus, look a sampling of the reviews: are many of them generic ("He's a great attorney!"), or do they contain case-specific details? The more generic they are, especially if there's a lot of generics, the more likely the attorney is paying for the reviews – steer clear.

CONCLUSION:
WHAT'S THE NEXT STEP?

Ok – so now you're ready to file your case and you're ready to shop for an attorney well-armed with information – what now?

Star gathering the information and documents you and your attorney will need for the case. Verify the legal names you used to get married form your marriage certificate. Verify the father's name is on any of the children's birth certificates.

Start researching the values of any properties – if you've had a recent appraisal done (e.g., via a mortgage refinance), get a copy of same to your attorney. Verify from the deeds/titles whose names are on each property, vehicle, account, etc. Bring a copy of the deeds/titles and the most recent financial account statements in to your attorney. Produce a copy of your most recent retirement account statement to your attorney.

Start thinking about whether you're willing to settle for some form of joint custody for the kids – and what access schedule you'd agree to. Is relocation an issue – and if so, what are the parameters of same?

Give thought to how you'd like assets and debts divided, as well as whether you feel you need spousal maintenance (if you're the less-monied spouse). If you're the more-monied spouse, start thinking about whether you'd like to request a reduction from the guidelines amounts – and if so, how much & why?

As the case proceeds, keep your own folder containing all the relevant case documents, including court filings your attorney gives to you, copies of the pertinent financial records as well as copies of correspondence exchanged between yourself & your attorney. More than a few times I've been in court and a client says "I thought I had given you that document" – and when I say they hadn't, it would've been helpful for them to simply grab it from their own case folder s/he brought with them.

If you have a need for interim orders – such as interim order of exclusive occupancy of the marital residence, an order of protection, and/or interim orders of custody, visitation, child support, maintenance or counsel fees, discuss this with your attorney. Don't let it go or assume this will just magically happen on its own.

You should refrain from posting things on social media about the case and/or your soon-to-be-ex-spouse. But do not delete anything which is already there – it *may* be construed as you trying to get rid of evidence.

You're entitled to receive copies of all pertinent documents and correspondence on the case form your lawyer – if you don't receive something you think you should, speak up! You should also receive an itemized billing invoice from your lawyer once every 30-60 days so you can keep track of how much is coming out of your account (even if you don't currently owe money) or how much your balance is.

Most lawyers in this field bill in increments of .1 – meaning a minimum of 6 minutes per task, which in turn is usually rounded up to the next highest 6-minutes. Bear this in mind before sending your lawyer 10 e-mails in one day – you're generally billed separately for each & every task, meaning receipt & review of each separate e-mail or phone call.

Furthermore, you must generally physically appear in court on each court date, unless otherwise advised by your lawyer or the Judge. Do not assume merely because you've hired an attorney s/he can just "do the case for me!"

Additionally, if you disagree with any given order or decision of the Judge in your case, discuss immediately with your lawyer when you should appeal. There is generally a deadline of 30 days from receipt of any given order to file your notice of appeal (35 days if mailed). And usually this deadline cannot be extended!

Do not disappear on your lawyer – if you change your contact information at all (new phone, new e-mail, etc), be sure your attorney is given same.

Also, if your case becomes contested, there's no need to call your lawyer if you forgot when your court date is. You may also track your case status and ascertain the next court date by accessing New York Court system's e-court page WebCivilSupreme at:

http://iapps.courts.state.ny.us/webcivil/FCASMain. On this website, you may also access e-track so you may receive e-mail notifications of your next court date and well as updated case status reports.

Moreover, the proper role of an attorney is to assist you with your case – but always keep in mind it's *your case*. This means because you have a stake in the outcome, you need to be an active participant in the proceedings. Among other things, this means offering to assist your lawyer by doing drafts of needed affidavits on your own, completing spreadsheets of your finances – and making appointments early & often to discuss your case with your lawyer. The more at stake, the more often you should meet with your lawyer. At the least, you should have an appointment with him/her prior to each scheduled court date (or offer to do so & allow your lawyer to say "nah, it's not necessary").

Finally, help your attorney help you! Be realistic and do not expect your lawyer to deliver you the sun, the moon & the stars. Most divorce case (90%+) result in a settlement. And most settlements, in turn, involve compromise on both party's behalf. Thus, each party to the case usually gives up something which s/he feels otherwise entitled to. Know that if the law is against you on certain issues, your lawyer can't change the law – the only thing s/he can do is argue an exception. And exceptions, by their very nature, are unlikely to succeed.

Following these recommendations will serve to relieve stress, save money and ensure your case goes as efficiently as possible. All the best!

ABOUT THE AUTHOR

David Bliven graduated with honors from Syracuse University in 1993 with a B.A. in Sociology. He went on to serve as a judicial intern and statistician with the NYS Commission on City Court Judicial Reallocation with the Office of the Deputy Chief Administrative Judge. He then attended New York Law School where he graduated in 1997 with honors and ranked within the top 15% of his class.

Upon graduation, he worked in private practice for a year (doing mostly matrimonial work), before serving as a prosecutor for nearly 3 years with the NYC

Administration for Children's Services. While at ACS he prosecuted child support, child abuse & neglect and foster care cases on behalf of the City of New York.

After leaving the prosecutor position, Mr. Bliven opened his present practice in 2000. His philosophy is to provide quality legal representation at affordable prices. His practice is approximately 99% divorce & Family Court cases, along with 1% governmental misconduct and administrative cases.

Mr Bliven has an "AV" rating from Martindale-Hubbell (the highest possible rating in both Legal Ability & Ethical Standards), a perfect 10.0 rating from Avvo ("Superb" rating) and is listed in the "Super Lawyers" directory by Thompson Reuters (a distinction given to less than 5% of all attorneys in each field of practice).

Mr. Bliven also authors "Cases That Help" - an annual caselaw newsletter distributed to Family Court Assigned Counsel panels throughout the State of New York, and his articles have been published in the New York Law Journal.

TESTIMONIALS

- Hector M.: "David's expertise in the area of law in which I needed representation was far superior to what my previous lawyers had given me, considering the higher than average fees they wanted, David came in at a reasonable price, and again his knowledge of the law in my case was outstanding!! I would hire him again, and definitely recommend David to friends and family."

- Jose P.: "Awesome loved working with attorney David Bliven. Hope that I don't need him anymore but if I need one he will be it."

- Juvy J.: "I am well satisfied with him in regards to all my questions. He very well answered everything I asked."

- Randel Y.: "Responded to my case in a professional manner."

- Jason W.: "I couldn't ask for a better lawyer"

- Mark B: "My first day in court my wife wanted spousal support and he find a way to stop it, David definitely knows what he's doing."

- David M.: "David handled my 'no-fault' divorce case before 'no-fault' existed in the state of New York with ease, transparency, and efficiency. I vetted a lot of different lawyers and he was the best."

- Daniel C.: "I will rehired [sic] him anytime when it come down to it!!!!!"

- Peter S.: "Mr Bliven was very professional, knowledgeable and responded to all my question in a timely fashion. He made it Simple to understand all the legal language. A Glimmer of light throughout a Dark legal battle. I am very grateful for all his hard work. Will definitely recommend."

- Bharrat S.: "He finished the case in the first appearance and less than 15 minutes."

****

More Testimonials may be found on Mr Bliven's website (http://www.blivenlaw.net/Testimonials.shtml) and at Avvo (https://www.avvo.com/attorneys/10463-ny-david-bliven-952796.html#client_reviews).

INDEX

T

V

NOTES